DK

A Dorling Kindersley Book

Written by Mary Atkinson
Art Editor Mandy Earey
Deputy Managing Editor Dawn Sirett
Deputy Managing Art Editor
C. David Gillingwater
Production Josie Alabaster
Picture Research Angela Anderson

First published in Great Britain in 1997
by Dorling Kindersley Limited,
9 Henrietta Street, London WC2E 8PS

Visit us on the World Wide Web at http://www.dk.com

Copyright © 1997 Dorling Kindersley Limited, London

A CIP catalogue record for this book is
available from the British Library.

ISBN 0-7513-5600-X

Colour reproduction by Chromagraphics, Singapore
Printed and bound in Italy by L.E.G.O.

The publisher would like to thank the following for their kind
permission to reproduce their photographs:

t=top, b=bottom, l=left, r=right, c=centre, BC=back cover, FC=front cover

Format Photographers: Jacky Chapman 20 bl; **Robert Harding Picture Library:**
11br, 16bl, 16-17c, 18-19c; **The Image Bank:** 14bl; **Images Colour Library:** 6tl;
Tony Stone Images: Charles Thatcher endpapers, Bob Thomas 8bl,
Chip Henderson FC c, 10tl, Andy Sacks 10-11c, Pascal Crapet BC c, 12-13c,
14-15c, Mitch Kezar 13br, Ian Shaw 12tl, Steven Peters 17br;
Zefa: 6-7c, 9tr, 19br, 20-21c.

Additional photography by John Garrett, Ray Moller,
Susannah Price, Jules Selmes, and Kim Taylor.

Contents

Why do Mum and Dad's
hugs feel so good? 6

Why do I feel shy when I
meet new friends? 8

Why can't I be happy
all the time? 10

Why do I get cross with
other people? 12

Why do I cry when
I'm feeling sad? 14

Why are some people scared
of mice or spiders? 16

Why do people jump and shout
when they're excited? 18

Why do I feel left out now
that we have a new baby? 20

WHY

can't I be happy all the time?

Questions children ask
about feelings

Consultant: Diane Melvin, Clinical Child Psychologist

DK

DORLING KINDERSLEY

London • New York • Stuttgart • Moscow • Sydney

Why do Mun

A hug from Mum and Dad
is one way they let us know
how much they love us.
Hugs can make us feel saf

**Why do we love the people
in our family so much?**
The people in our family are
usually the people we share
our lives with. They look
after us when we're growing
up, and so we love them a
lot. Although sometimes we
feel cross with them, at other
times we realize how much
we care about them.

and Dad's hugs feel so good?

...nd cared for. They can ...ay goodnight, or good ...norning, have a happy ...lay, or welcome home.

Why do Mum and Dad tell me off if they love me?
When grown-ups tell us off they are usually thinking about what's best for us. They want to stop us doing anything dangerous. They also want us to learn not to be rude or selfish so that we'll get on well with others and feel happy.

Why do I feel shy when

Lots of children feel shy around other children they don't know. It takes time to get to know people and to trust them as friends. Often, we worry less about this as we grow older and so don't feel as shy.

Why do I feel homesick when I stay with friends? Staying overnight with friends can be great fun, but occasionally we all feel homesick. Every family is different. Often, we miss our own family and the usual things we do when we're at home.

I meet new friends?

Why do I sometimes feel lonely?
Everyone feels lonely now and again. It happens particularly when friends leave us out or when those we love are busy or away. At times like this, we feel as if other people don't care about us. Finding a quiet time to tell them about how we feel can help us sort things out.

Why can't

When good things happen, we feel full of happiness. When bad things happen, we feel sad. Most of the

Why can silly games be so much fun?
Most of us enjoy letting go and being silly once in a while. Laughing and playing harmless games can be good for us, too. They help us to relax and can take our minds off any problems we might have.

I be happy all the time?

time, however, we just feel okay. We can probably feel happy more if we don't let unimportant things upset us.

Why do I feel good when I help other people? Making other people feel happy can make us feel happy, too. By thinking about others and helping them, we start to know them better – and we might even become good friends!

Why do I get

When people do things that we don't like or that we think are unfair, it can make us feel cross. Sharing

Why do people shout when they're cross?
When people are angry, they sometimes shout to make other people stop and listen. Shouting can help us to get out our angry feelings and start to feel better. Sometimes, however, it is rude to shout. For instance, shouting in class would disturb your classmates.

cross with other people?

our feelings with people we trust can help us sort them out before they build up and we feel even angrier.

Why do difficult things make me so frustrated?
Sometimes when we can't see an easy way to solve a problem, it makes us feel frustrated. We are annoyed with ourselves because we can't work out what to do.

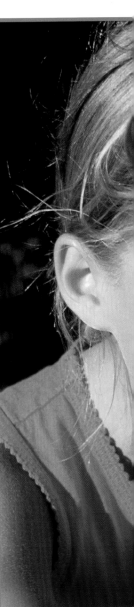

Storing unhappy feelings inside ourselves doesn't make them go away. Crying is our body's way of helping us to let out unhappy feelings and to start feeling better. It also lets other people know that something is wrong.

Why do I feel sad when Mum is sad?
When we love people, we feel upset if they're sad. Sometimes there is nothing we can do to fix their problems, but just knowing we care can help them to feel better.

eeling sad?

Why did my dog have to die?
All animals and people die eventually. Often they die when their bodies wear out in old age, but sometimes an illness or accident means they die while they're still young. When a pet or person dies, we feel very sad. After a while, however, we're able to enjoy remembering them and the things we used to do with them.

Our feelings don't always make sense. Sometimes we feel scared of things that aren't really dangerous. A mouse, for example, couldn't hurt a person, yet many people scream in fright if they see one.

Why does the dark scare me?
In the dark, we can't see what's happening around us. It's easy to imagine all sorts of scary things that aren't really there. But when we turn on a light, we can see that a lurking monster is really a tree or a chair.

scared of mice or spiders?

Why are new things so scary?
When we start a new school, join a club, or try something else that's new, we often feel afraid of what will happen. We soon settle in, however, and our fears start to disappear. As we do more and more new things, we usually feel more confident.

Why do people jump and

When we're full of excitement and happiness, running about and shouting for joy are ways we let loose our emotions and show others how we feel. Expressing our happy feelings helps us to enjoy good times even more.

Why can't I open my presents before my birthday?
People give you birthday presents to make your birthday a special day. If you opened your presents before your birthday, you wouldn't have any surprises on the day.

shout when they're excited?

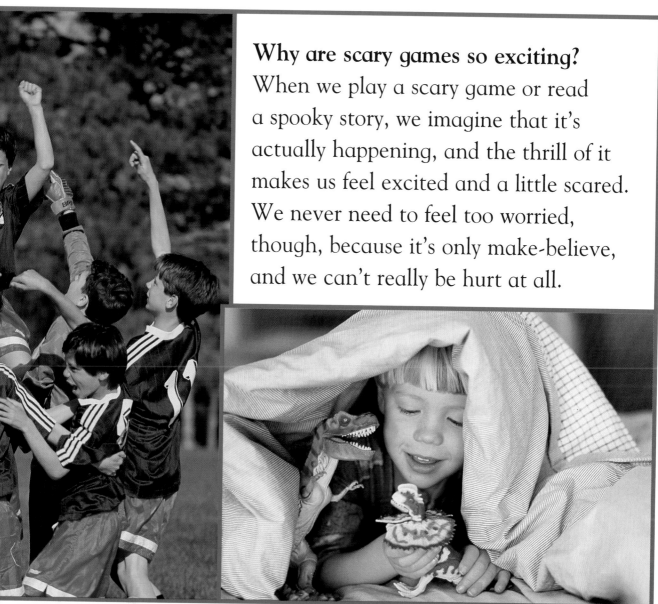

Why are scary games so exciting?
When we play a scary game or read
a spooky story, we imagine that it's
actually happening, and the thrill of it
makes us feel excited and a little scared.
We never need to feel too worried,
though, because it's only make-believe,
and we can't really be hurt at all.

Why do I feel left out now

Why does my friend want to play with someone else?
Sometimes our friends enjoy playing with other people or making new friends. This can make us feel jealous. It might help to tell your friends how you feel. See if you can join in or ask another friend to play with you instead.

When your parents are bus with a new baby, you may think they have no time for you. But your parents still

that we have a new baby?

...vant to do things with you.
...hey just need to give extra
...ime to a baby because it
...an't look after itself.

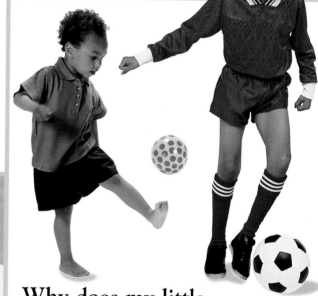

**Why does my little
brother always copy me?**
When someone copies you
it's because they like you and
admire you. They think that
if they do what you do, they
can be just like you. Although
this can be annoying, it's also
very flattering.